FRAGRANT WORDS

FRAGRANT WORDS

RAJNI SEKHRI SIBAL

Illustrated by

TK MANOJ KUMAR

B L O O M S B U R Y

NEW DELHI • LONDON • OXFORD • NEW YORK • SYDNEY

BLOOMSBURY INDIA
Bloomsbury Publishing India Pvt. Ltd
Second Floor, LSC Building No. 4, DDA Complex, Pocket C – 6 & 7,
Vasant Kunj, New Delhi 110070

BLOOMSBURY, BLOOMSBURY PRIME and the Diana logo are
trademarks of Bloomsbury Publishing Plc

First published in 2019

ISBN: 978-93-88912-77-8

4 6 8 10 9 7 5 3

Cover painting by Uma Singh
Copyright of Pen and Ink Illustrations: TK Manoj Kumar
Printed and bound in India by Replika Press Pvt Ltd

To find out more about our authors and books, visit
www.bloomsbury.com and sign up for our newsletters

For
Lakshi and Pushan

About all the beautiful people
who have enriched my life.
About all the beautiful moments
that make life special...

NOTE FROM THE AUTHOR

Words have a way of flowing along the path they choose. They often leave behind a trail that is fragrant. Some words are soft and gentle, some harsh and stark and some evoke the aroma of a memory long forgotten.

Like the brilliant strokes of a painter, words paint pictures that display the various colours on a poet's palette – the black, the white and the mesmerising hues in between. A little like life.

Fragrant Words is a journey through life—the misty, the sunny and the harsh. This anthology of verses is a collection of words that have been strung together over the years.

I write without a plan and I write as I feel. Sometimes I cannot stop the flow of words and hurriedly put pen to paper in the strangest of places: by the side of a tempestuous lake in the monsoon, outside a quaint shop amid the labyrinthine lanes of an ancient city, under a fragrant magnolia tree at the edge of a forest, behind my folder at the end of a long drawn discussion and in the space beside screaming headlines of the morning paper.

After *Clouds End and Beyond*, published in 2017, *Fragrant Words* is my second anthology. The verses in *Fragrant Words* depict all the colours of the rainbow: dreamy vistas blurred by harsh realities, mellow calmness disrupted by loud cacophony and beautiful emotions tempered with teardrops in the rain.

This anthology comprises of verses that are wistful and reminiscent of rosy sunsets and a walk amid aromatic pine trees and purple mountains. Quaint, picturesque villages in the Himalayas and charming old towns like Kasauli and Mussoorie are the backdrop against which the more misty and aromatic words evolved. 'A Winter's Day', 'And the Hills Come Alive', 'Morning has Broken' and 'Gypsy Wanderings' fall into this dreamy theme.

The anthology also contains works which emote and touch silken chords like the memory of a father in 'The End of an Era' and the warmth of the precious relationship between mothers and daughters in 'An Eloquent Affection' and in 'As You Will'. The verses 'If Only' and 'Orchids and Daisies' are rather wistful and a poignant thread runs through verses like 'Strangers over Time' who are 'There Yet Not There' as well as 'Distant Souls', written for a friend who died before her time.

The theme of tender emotional bonds which include mystical offerings that travel beyond the horizon can be found in compositions like: 'The Ethereal Strain', 'Magnolia Offerings', 'Cosmic Presence' and 'Mystic Music'.

The streets of Delhi are the stimulus for 'Chandni Chowk', 'A Concrete Life', 'Arranged Marriages', 'Lazy Sundays', 'Mountain's Call', 'Of Vultures and Blue Jays' and 'The Ragpicker'.

A cold winter in Moscow was the raison d'etre of the verses 'Mislaid by the Wind' and 'Siberia'.

Some of the compositions have been drawn from events that moved me. 'No Pain No More' conveys the unspeakable pain of a child eight-year-old who was raped and then killed. The dead child describes her ordeal to her mother through the poem. 'Coloured Vision' relates the story of a coloured youth beaten up by a group of strangers in a distant land where he was suspected of being a criminal because of the colour of his skin. These works are typical of verses that I have penned down in the space around the headlines of a newspaper.

'The Tsunami' portrays the immense tragedy of a natural disaster and was written on the ravaged shores of the Arabian Sea in Puducherry after the 2004 tsunami. The suffering and the non-violent battle of the homeless people from Tibet led by the Dalai Lama is painted in 'A Nation in Exile'.

Compositions like 'Annual Inspections', 'Meaningless Meetings', '…And a Contract is Made', 'Argumentative Minds' and 'Influential Indifference' depict the humdrum everyday life in a city and issues that are less esoteric.

The verses 'Fragrant Words', 'Verse with no Rhyme' and 'Remnant Verses' often question life and the new world order. The poem 'The Endangered List' illustrates how the very existence of words, verses and books is in danger as other modes of communication become more relevant in a world that has no time for poetry.

The anthology also portrays the enigma related to an inner quest in verses like 'Paradoxes', 'I am I matter', 'When the Snow Arrives Early', 'A World that is One', 'Blank Cosmos' and 'Where is Life Taking Me'.

Friends suggested that the compositions should be categorised and arranged in a more orderly manner. I like to leave them as is – a motley representation of what life brings…and without any order.

I would like to thank TK Manoj Kumar, a friend and a colleague in the Indian Administrative Service, for highlighting my words so artistically with his beautiful pen-and-ink pictures and the vignettes sketched by him. The sketches add depth to the anthology. I also place on record my gratitude to Uma Singh for allowing me to use her beautiful painting for the cover. Uma is an Indian Revenue Service (IRS) officer and a childhood friend. We went to Welham School together. The painting literally sings 'fragrance'.

This book is for all those who love poetry and believe in their dreams. It is also for those who are special to me and for the two persons who bring fragrance to my life – my children, Lakshi and Pushan.

Welcome, enter my world of *Fragrant Words*.

CONTENTS

MYSTIC MUSIC

Across the stream
Come play the flute—
My heart's a-sway
To your dulcet tune;

As the sun goes down
Come play again—
My feet tap time
To a magical strain;

Your breath so mellow
Your fingers entice—
Each note is pure
The song beguiles;

On a full moon night
Near a jasmine tree—
Your mystic notes
Set my soul free;

I sway like a dervish
I dance without care—
Your flute captivates
It captures and snares;

Play the final *mantra*
As I take my last breath—
Ease my leave-taking
… Harmony unto death.

EXPANSIVE INNER PEACE

The profound silence
Of a tranquil mind;
Like a deep blue lake
With placid banks.

The echoes of a valley
Dew-damp pine trees;
Misty purple mountains
Spicy mountain breeze.

Fireflies in the forest
Illumine shadowy roads;
Distant unseen vistas
Haunting unsung notes.

Heady lyrical music
Gentle rhythmic chants;
Heads bent down in prayer
The strength of folded hands.

Languid earthy fragrance
Of mingled mud and rain;
Potent perfumed incense
Forgotten sun-burnt pain.

The fluid calm activity
Of an actively calm sea;

Hues of a latent sunrise
Ambrosial morning tea.

A trail amidst the mountains
A voyage across the seas;
The rainbow ends within me
…In expansive inner peace.

ARGUMENTATIVE MINDS

The cynical sneer
Of a know it all,
Puffed with pride
Before a fall;

Louder the voice
Baser the content,
Skewed information
And angular intent;

Sly shifty eyes
Lie with ease,
A honeyed tongue
All eager to please;

Slanted statistics
Partisan opinions,
Cantankerous voices
Whimpering minions;

Debates are petty
The discussions blind,
Inconclusive meetings
Of argumentative minds.

A CONCRETE LIFE

Steel grey skies
Curdled smog
A jaded sun
Behind the fog
Starless nights
Leafless logs
Sulphur rain
Acidic drops…

My eyes smart
And spirits seethe
Please let me out
I cannot breathe.

Toxic roofs
Plastic paths
Airless caverns
Crowded marts
Synthetic cities
Bitumen warts
Stunted robots
Stony hearts…

My eyes smart
And spirits seethe
Please let me out
I cannot breathe.

No summer breeze
No glistening stars
No verdant trees
No fragrant flowers
To work and back
And back to work
No time to lose
No reminiscent hours…

My eyes smart
And spirits seethe
Please let me out
I cannot breathe.

No thought no words
A daily drill
A frantic dash
To nowhere-ville
A weary space
A tedious mill
A concrete life
No wish no will…

My eyes smart
And spirits seethe
Please let me out
I cannot breathe.

No time to read
No words to write
No tales to tell

Just dusty files
The mock concern
In ice-cold eyes
A concrete life
And sketchy smiles…

My eyes smart
And spirits seethe
Please let me out
I cannot breathe.

GYPSY WANDERINGS

Misty mornings—
Crisp as indigo,
Familiar tidings
A resounding echo.

Sitar strings—
A tug at the heart,
Forgotten yearnings
Time to depart.

Strange surroundings—
An alluring sound,
Gypsy wanderings
Homeward bound…

VERSE WITH NO RHYME

Scratched etchings on paper
Poignant words and phrases
Painted strokes of nostalgia
And déjà vu mellow traces…

– Of days gone by
– Of moments in space
– Of misty mountains
– Of forgotten faces.

The prose all out of sync
A verse without rhyme
The soft music of silence
Now dusty with time...

– As myths come true
– As the fog clears away
– As dreams float afar
– As reason comes to stay.

The dawn slides into dusk
The road is near its end
Summer changes seasons
There's no time to amend…

– The errors sweet as sin
– The quest yet incomplete
– The paths not yet trod
– On tired weary feet.

END OF AN ERA

The warmth of a fading lamp
The touch of his cashmere shawl
The crash of a giant oak:
And an era comes to an end.

From the glare of his pyre
From the embers and the ash
From his child to an adult:
The transition occurs too soon.

As one day follows another
As months slip into years
As memories stay and haunt:
A tear slides down unwittingly.

While a face become hazy
While a voice fades with time
While his books begin to age:
A father is missed each day.
...Every day.

Delhi Gate

CHANDNI CHOWK

Crumbling
Jharokhas
Cracked
Walls—
Timeless
Presence
Empty
Halls—
Winding
Lanes
Echoing
Domes—
Whispering
Arches
Unlived
Homes.

Fragrant
Names
Forgotten
Faces—
Moonlit
Nights
Elusive
Places—
Ancient
Books

Antique
Tales—
Tarnished
Silver
Distress
Sales.
Archaic
Lineage
Dusty
Dawn—
Erstwhile
Nawaabs
Compelled
To
Pawn—
The
Family
Silver
Treasured
Bowls
Forgotten
Lifestyles
Fractured
Souls.

History
Evolves
Again
Anew—
To a

Diverse
And
Altered
Worldview—
Quaint Winding
Lanes
Lean—
To
Greet
The
Vibrant
New
Bustling
Rainbow
Streets.

Where
Crossroads
Play
Hide
And
Seek—
With
The
Shimmering
Moon's
Silver
Streaks—
Where
Timeless

Grandfather
Clocks—
And
Ageleless
Bygone
Epochs
Join
The
Festive
Crowds
To
celebrate
A moonlit cross…
The resplendent Chandni Chowk.

THE TSUNAMI

Lonesome homeless
Vacant eyes
– Distraught.

Bustling villages
Swept asunder
– Devastated.

Trees and homes
Alive and dead
– Ravaged.

Screaming infants
Silent carcasses
– Lifeless.

Unlived lives
Man and beast
– Conquered.

Watery graves
Unlit pyres
– Extinguished.

And then
There is an eerie silence:
As the tsunami ebbs away…

NOT YET DONE

They tell me I am older
I've nothing more to do,
A little less to live
Nothing more to prove.
No stream to swim upstream
No snowy peaks to climb,
No upward growth in valour
A steady slow decline.

They tell me to stop dreaming
Of dreams that still remain,
To rest upon my laurels
And tally the loss and gain.
No music in the air
No rainbows left to follow,
No verses in the sky
A dreary lonesome hollow.

I hear with trepidation
Words that mock and warn,
Then hold my head up high
And say, 'I'm not yet done'.
'No time to hang my boots
No time to cease the strife,
No way I'll quit on living
A life so full of life'.

'I'm not yet done' I say
'I'm not yet done' I cry,
'I'll live a life worth living
I'll live until I die'.
No dull monotonous days
I'm not yet done with life
No way I'll quit on living
A life so full of life.

MORNING HAS BROKEN

Amber hues
Filter through
Inky clouds—
And tiptoe across
Sleep-laden
Dreamy eyes.

Sparrows land
On my window-sill
Chirp an alarm—
Heralding hope of
Another day
Another chance.

The aroma of roses
Bathed in dew
Is overpowered—
By the swirls of
Coffee waltzing up
To tingle my senses awake.

…Morning has broken.

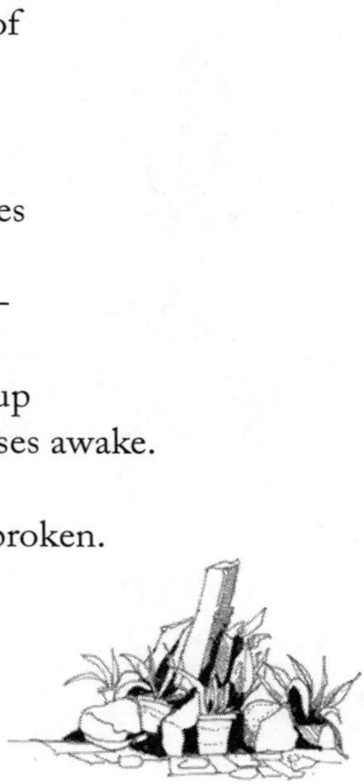

...AND A CONTRACT IS MADE

Stakeholder consultations
Fundamental chores;
You scratch my back
While I scratch yours.

Partners in returns
Of mutual assistance;
Competitive advantages
Of collaborative systems.

Dedicated infrastructure
On subsidised rates;
The exclusive domains
Of symbiotic mates.

Productive discussions
And negotiated trade;
Present the presentation
...And a contract is made.

STRANGERS OVER TIME

Breathless sudden encounters
Of strangers over time,
Suspended conversations
Like verses with no rhyme.

Eyes that do not meet
To hide the hidden pain,
Lips begin to quiver
Unspoken words again.

Questions never asked
A good deal left unsaid,
Countless years apart
Diverse paths to tread.

Let us forget the past
Forgive the mutual pain,
And meet without baggage
Like strangers once again…

ENDANGERED LIST

Words
That flow
Like the falling rain;
Words
That melt
Like snow in vain;
Words
Are windows
To a world within;
Words
Are trails
Of tales they spin;
Some words
When spoken
Can damage
And harm
Some words
When whispered
Can soothe
And calm
Words
I read
And
Words
I write
Who cares—
Who reads?

Who cares—
Who writes?
For prose
And verse
And books
And words
Are now on the endangered list.

REMINISCENT SMILES

When the forest calls
When the clouds part
When the sky is cerulean blue;
When the air is crisp
When flowers bloom
A song reminds me of you.

The time stops still
As the years slip by
The distance disappears;
The forgotten phase
The unlived dreams
A reminiscent smile appears.

Of breathless words
Of ruffled hair
Of a caring without care;
Of timeless times
Of misty moments
A treasure trove so rare.

As time moves on
As paths diverge
As they never cross again;
As reality stares
As memories fade
A teardrop mingles with rain.

The echoes of a distant age
The touch of a mellow breeze
The aroma of a summer shower;
The hues of autumn trees
The soft glow of a firefly
A book-marked with a flower.

...Memoirs of a forgotten phase
And a reminiscent smile appears.

OF VULTURES AND BLUE JAYS

A sparkling blue jay
In a dull grey grove
Incongruent amongst
Vultures and crows
Heckled and worn
All pecked and torn
With broken wings
Yet a spirit strong
Cacophonic caws
And sharp-hooked beaks
All ready to claw
And tear and tweak
She bides her time
No whimper no moan
Then gathers her wings
Towards the unknown
Above cumulus clouds
Beyond the humdrum
With sparkling wings
She reaches for the sun.

WHEN THE SNOW ARRIVES EARLY

When one door shuts
And no window opens
I search the ether for light;
When the sun goes down
And the dark descends
The stars are not too bright:
The subtle glow of an earthen lamp
...Lights up the moonless night.

When the snow arrives
Before summer is done
And my world is upside down;
When the earth rotates
Before I find my feet
And life becomes undone:
I rest awhile and contemplate
...And calm descends anon.

When sunny days go
Never to come back
The angst stays awhile;
When the heart desires
And the mind acquiesces
It's tough to reconcile:
I let the past go and go with the flow
...And grow with every strife.

When the clouds burst open
In an intense thunderstorm
The downpour mingles with tears;
When nothing seems right
In a world gone wrong
And hope fades into fears:
I shut my eyes and gaze within
...And serenity engulfs my being.

When one door shuts
And no window opens
I search the ether for light;
When the sun goes down
As the dark descends
And stars are not too bright:
The subtle glow of an earthen lamp
...Lights up the moonless night.

ARRANGED MARRIAGES

A crowd of strangers
Portraits exchanged
Shy fleeting glances
Reticent and restrained

Crimson hued cheeks
Like the ashes of a rose
Dangling conversations
Austere poetic prose

The families congregate
Common links are found
Horoscopes get matched
A mutual meeting ground

Destined by the stars
Ordained over tea
Partners for a lifetime
Who dare disagree?

A *pundit* is essential
To fix the wedding date,
Bedeck a hall, bejewel the bride
Before it is too late

Prepare saffron sweets
Invite *all* the gods
Beat the booming *dhol*
Expunge all the odds.

There's *henna* and *haldi*
And festivity galore
Song dance and colour
The *bhangra* and more.

The bride in bright red
Behind a gossamer veil,
Charming and exquisite
Yet nervous and pale.

The *shehnai* drowns down
Her choked unheard voice
A soft anxious whisper
'Do *I* have no choice?'

A right to say: 'Wait:
Is *he* the right man?
Is *this* the right time?
Is this what *I* want?'
She peers through the gloss
And hears above the din
The unheard inner voice
The unspoken revolt within.

'Stop the loud music!
Take off your dancing shoes!
Remove my stuffy veil!
I want the right to choose!'

MEANINGLESS MEETINGS

Formal greetings
Unending discussions
Dialectic dialogues
Underlying currents;
Subdued turmoil and
Placid anxiety that
Skirts the issue with
Wordless verbosity;
Dogged arguments
Rhetoric questions
Shaky foundations
Mindless interjections;
The clock ticks on
And dinner is served
The meeting concludes
With meaningless words.

ORCHIDS AND DAISIES

A new dawn heralds hope
That fades when dusk is near
Like life that's full of life
Till clouds begin to appear.

Some ties obey the rules
While others have no name
Orchids need to be nurtured
While daisies grow un-tame.

Some souls belong together
Yet tread divergent trails
Like paths that meet at crossroads
Then go their separate ways.

Like skies that blush at sunset
Till the shadows cover all
Like the citrus green of spring
Turns dusky brown in fall.

Some images appear so perfect
At a distance seem profound
As the sun clears up the mist
They prove to be unsound.

Sometimes I sit in silence
Far from the madding band

I hear the unheard sounds
And seek to understand…

Why rules define some ties
While others have no name?
Why orchids need to be nurtured
While daisies grow untamed?

ELOQUENT AFFECTION

We're two soulmates
Both I and you
Linked with the past
And our futures too.

I dreamt each night
Of your dainty feet
Your tiny fingers
Enticingly sweet.

Your beautiful face
Your innocent smile
Ensnared for ever
Besotted for life.

Of mothers and daughters
A resilient connection
Soft silken strings
An eloquent affection.

I'll stay by your side
In pleasure and woe
Through sun and rain
Together we'll grow.

Let's reach for the stars
Whatever the weather
The world will be ours
Together – forever.

Himalayas.

AND THE HILLS COME ALIVE

The sun's first rays
Touch and play tag amidst
Snow-peaked mountains
...And the hills come alive.

A crystal clear sky
Mirrors the calypso sea
Beckoning an aimless rambler
...And the hills call out to me.

A winding mountain trail
Meanders and disappears
Amid sun streaked foliage
...And the hills narrate a mystery.

Unheard melodies are sung
By unseen exotic birds
Atop unfamiliar alpine trees
...And the hills sing along.

Wild daisies and dahlias
Dance and sway in unison
On a verdant floral carpet
... And the hills stand witness.

The aroma of pine trees
Swirls up and engulfs

The core of my very being
...And the hills whisper my name.

A lucid magnetic call
Across jungles of concrete
Through crowded city streets
...And the hills entangle my soul.

THE ETHEREAL STRAIN

Across the river
Where the skies bend,
Over green meadows
Towards day's end;

When the sun goes down
And the sky turns red,
On unchecked feet
I scamper ahead;

My anklets a-tinkle
Beneath a mango tree,
On a full moon night
You play for me;

I hear the music
The notes flow free,
Magical and haunting
Like waves at sea;

Come play for me
In the monsoon rai
The earth is bathed
With fragrant pain;

Spin your magic
Come play again
The skies resound
To the ethereal strain.

BLANK COSMOS

Blank…
I came with nothing
My memory's a blank
Beyond the horizon
The cosmos is blank.

All my life's efforts
I package with care
Boxes of memories
My favourite ware
Evocative pieces
The glitter and glare
Small tender parcels
Fragrant and rare.

But…
I came with nothing
My memory's a blank
Beyond the horizon
The cosmos is blank.

So full of myself
A world of my own
An illusion I craft
I guard all I own:
My home, my life
My reputation too

My talent, my name
And all I deem true.

Yet…
I came with nothing
My memory's a blank
Beyond the horizon
The cosmos is blank.

The tighter I hold
The sooner it goes
The dearer it is
The higher it soars
I reach for the stars
On the tip of my toes
As I unclench my fist
Sheer emptiness flows.

For…
I came with nothing
My memory's a blank
Beyond the horizon
The cosmos is blank.

ANNUAL INSPECTIONS

Encrypted messages
Spread like fire
Launch preparations
Or face *Sahab's* ire—
It's time once again
For the annual inspections.

Jittery jeeps
Jostle along
Dusty roads
Awash with rain–
On the pristine morning
Of the annual inspection.

Coarse rest houses
Ancient chairs
Creaky-kneed
Ageing caretakers—
Spruce up the place
For the annual inspection.

White towels cover
Tattered upholstery
Fried cashew-nuts
And sickly-sweet tea—
All eager to please
At the annual inspection.

Folded palms
Greasy hair
Sugared tongues
And tense shifty eyes—
Behind lowered lashes
It's the annual inspection.

Shaky financials
Targets attained
Illusory growth
Progressive gain—
All neatly documented
For the annual inspection.

Rhetorical questions
Mumbled responses
Unexplained data
Deceptive nuances—
And the charade commences
At the annual inspection.

Customary tangos
Don't rock the boat
Ritual wrangles
Let's cover and coat—
Till it's time once again for
The next annual inspection.

COLOURED VISION

A clouded sea
Of angry faces
Towers over me
In unknown places;

Armed with hate
A vicious attack
For I am different
I was born Black;

A furious mob
Enraged and hot
My skin my mark
My colour my fault;

Brown and Black
Yellow and White
Shades skin-deep
Yet grounds to fight;

Stop the earth now
Or spin it around
Across the skies
And under the ground;

Come soar with me
Beyond the sun
Where colours don't matter
And every-one is one.

DISTANT SOULS

A time to remember
A day to reminisce
An uncharted journey
An unknown abyss.

A string of emotions
A moist fuzzy vision
As you part to go
To a new dimension.

A flurry of words
A tug at the heart
The skies turn grey
It's time to part.

Sooner or later
Go we all must
Beyond the horizon
And mingle with dust.

You're so far away
And yet so close
Friends for life
Now distant souls.

REMNANT VERSES

Forgotten names
Indulgent smiles
Stolen moments
All ribboned and wrapped.
Whispered venues
Profuse promises
Charming exchanges
Now saved and packed...

Tender words
Hazy faces
Lyrical notes
From a distant date.
Fragrant rains
Forgotten flowers
Remnant verses
In a dormant state...

A NATION IN EXILE

Cobalt blue skies
And crisp cold air
Hoary mountainsides
All rocky and bare.

Picture-perfect meadows
With daisies and weeds
Nothing to possess
Just small basic needs.

Simple hill folk
Both innocent and kind
Buddha's chosen few
And still in a bind.

A gentle middle path
Non-violent and true
Up against a storm
So bloody and blue.

Rule of the Gun
Obey and abide
Some live gagged
The rest in exile.

Dazed empty eyes
Banished by the gun

No path leads home
A nation on the run.

Hopes start a-fading
There's no end in sight
No sun this winter
No warmth – no light.

Homeless and weary
Dreams in despair
Moist vacant eyes
With a dismal glare.

Don't cry for Tibet
Her daughters and sons
A nation in exile
No place for guns.

No, don't cry for Tibet
Bow down and smile
Salute the brave hearts
Of a nation in exile.

PARADOXES

Incongruous alignment
Of the non-aligned;
Common norms
Of the non-common;

Meandering paths
That lead nowhere;
Rhetoric questions
That get no response;

Ornamental frippery
To bind the crack;
Inane platitudes
To ease the pain;

Haughty arrogance
And a flawed self-image;
Pugnacious violence
And a parade of power;

Muffled emancipated
Regimented voices;
And the fettered liberation
Of enchained souls;

Paradoxes!

THE MOUNTAIN'S CALL

The mountain's call
Comes over the stream
From a distant terrain
Revisits my dream;

Close to dawn
It echoes again
And flowers dance
To its lilting strain;

The air is crisp
Refreshing and sweet
The magnetic call
Draws my feet;

The world's asleep
But morning is near
This placid space
Will soon disappear;

The clamour and clutter
The hectic pace of life
Masks the pastoral call
And amplifies the strife;

As the city begins to stir
On a dreary grey day
The call of a mountain
Quietly fades away.

MISLAID BY THE WIND

Names and faces
Hazy with time;
Etch deep traces
In forlorn spaces
Like castles of sand…

Moon-lit flowers
With silver edges;
Sunshine showers
On rain-drenched bowers
Like a gossamer strand…

Verse and phrase
Mislaid by the wind;
Along a misty maze
Amid fog and haze
In a harsh stony land.

MAGNOLIA OFFERINGS

Beneath the stars
Your music flows,
The forest's a-sway
To a dulcet glow;

Behind the clouds
You play again,
The wind sings along
To a mystic strain;

The earth resonates
With a song exquisite,
Each note is pure
The sky is all lit;

A pitch black night
And a thousand stars,
Resplendent like the
Magnolia flowers;

The flowers that I offer
As I ring the temple bell,
Then light an earthen lamp
And blow the conch shell;

Magnolia offerings
In a carved silver bowl
Magnolia offerings
With a touch of my soul.

I AM – AND I MATTER

I am not the person who kills
Because your views are profane,
Nor am I a frenzied fanatic
Who shoots in god's name;
No dogmas confine my soul:
...For I am non-judgemental.

I am neither Black nor White
Nor Yellow, Red or Brown,
My colour is skin-deep
It does not define me;
Nor does it colour my vision:
...For I cherish the rainbow.

I am not the crusader who questions
Every stance that differs from mine,
Nor do I believe that what I hold
Is the one and only truth sublime;
A black-and-white world is not for me:
...For I follow my own dreams.

I am a miniscule speck in time
Invisible on the larger canvas,
An innocuous part of the cosmos
Here today – gone tomorrow;
But even as I embrace the ether:
I leave footprints in the sand of time.

For I matter.
I *am* matter.
I am – and I matter.

A WORLD THAT IS ONE

A long time ago
The world was one
No divisive borders
No hate – no gun;
As sagas unfolded
Before the sun rose
There was no light
No verse – no prose;
The skies were dark
No respite in sight
No song – no flower
No wrong – nor right;
An unending trudge
Along endless roads
No tree – no hearth
Just dreary shadows.

Then dawn arrived
And cleansed the air
The seasons in the sun
Purged the despair;
Meadows and streams
A clear crisp breeze
Flowers and rainbows
And birds and trees.
There were no divisions
Neither class nor creed

No haste to possess
No hate – no greed;
There were hills to climb
And skies to soar
And stars to reach
To triumph and more.

But with one step forward
We took two behind
Realised our power
And lost our mind;
Forests were felled
And rivers defiled
Grab from nature
A race gone wild;
We created energy
And Hiroshima too
An atom gone awry
An inhuman zoo;
Shamed and maimed
We killed to win
A world at war
The enemy within.

Reprint the blueprint
Bridge the divide
Of class and colour
Of exclusive pride;
Let's learn to listen
Heal festering wounds

See through the bigots
Hypocrites and goons;
Let's join and restore
Each person her right:
To her body – her soul
And a dignified life;
Let's start to set right
The wrongs we've done
Return all we snatched
From a world that is one.

THE RAGPICKER

She's dressed in rags,
And collects garbage
She tidies the clutter
At a nominal wage;
She cleans and clears
She picks the rags,
She sweeps the lanes
And mops and drags;
Her absence is noticed
Her presence is not,
Her work elemental
She doesn't belong;
Can't live without her
Don't know her name
With averted eyes
Don't see her pain;
A picker in rags
She clears the mess
Her life's a drag
Her soul in distress...

The ragpicker and I
Aren't really apart
From nether we come
Unto naught we depart...

FRAGRANT WORDS

Words:
Evoke images
Of life and come alive;

Half-truth:
The fuzzy grey
Between the black and the white.

Love:
A heady feeling when
A baby clasps your finger.

Memory:
A tender moment
To savour and linger.

Colourful:
Painted rainbows
Which transform the skies.

Nostalgia:
A hazy image
Of soft resilient ties.

Autumn:
A russet breeze
That cools a blazing summer.

Rain-drops:
On showered leaves
That glisten and shimmer.

Dusk:
A blushing sky
That dons a shadowy veil.

Storm:
In a steamy teacup
All laced up with hale.

Zeal:
The avid fervour
Of a horse born wild;

Words:
Bequeath meaning
And fragrance to life.

NO PAIN NO MORE

No mother don't cry
Don't cry in vain
I'm beyond their reach
Past grief and pain.

Just shreds of meat
For hyenas in pants
I screamed with anger
I folded my hands.

I fought with my nails
I kicked and I whined
Dear mother I cried
For you as they dined.

They gorged on me
They gnawed and tore
Despite temple bells
They hurt me more.

Six filthy mouths?
Or ten ugly hands?
It's a painful blur
And I lost all count.

I suffered half dead
For several days

Revolting red blotches
In a dull grey haze.

Torn and defeated
I lay on the floor
My body a carcass
They came back for more.

I thought of you mother
As pain ebbed away
I dreamt of the meadows
Where we used to play.

You laughed as you ran
As I caught up you smiled
I smiled at the memory
And I smiled as I died.

Don't cry for me mother
I'm no longer sore
No Hyenas – no Vultures
No pain – No more.

OF BIRDS AND SAPIENS

The crows raucously
Squabble over the inane,
As Sparrows chirp
And twitter in unison;
A Puffin puffs up
With pompous pride and
A Peacock struts around
With arrogant derision.

The Tailorbird toils
To build a warm home,
While a Cuckoo coos
Over the spoils;
A Kookaburra laughs
In his old gum tree
As he watches
The others toil.

An Eagle flies
Above the foggy clouds,
As the Hawk
Scrutinises the divide;
Biding her time
With muscles tense
To swoop with alacrity
Then snatch and hide.

Her eyes affixed
The Hawk awaits,
The Eagle encircles
A hundred miles;
The Vulture scorns
And sneers in disdain
Aware and bolstered that
Eventually the carrion is his.

INFLUENTIAL INDIFFERENCE

Case under submission
Work in progress,
Circuitous arguments
—Without any basis.

Meetings, discussions
Endless debates,
Apathetic dialogues
—As logic abates.

Raucous cacophony
Grotesque and gross,
Listless responses
—Festering sores.

Parroted words
Without reflection,
Relentless arrogance
—Tunnelled vision.

Unheard cries
Invisible pain,
Justice delayed
—Denied again.

Investigations close
Without any gain,
A solitary verdict…
—To enquire again.

THERE—YET NOT THERE

You are there—yet not there:
For you're there in my thoughts
You're therein my dreams
You come as you will
You go as you please
Like a watery sun
And untimely showers
Like brown autumn leaves
And mid-summer flowers
As a cloud floats away
At the stir of a breeze
As the last leaf falls
And bares the trees
You are there—and yet not there.

You are there—yet not there:
When the clouds descend
In gloomy despair
Through thick and thin
Through rough and fair
You come by my side
From wherever you are
You're always there
But somewhere far
Like the golden sound
Of silken strings
Like the whispered magic

A melody brings
You are there – and yet not there.

You are there – yet not there:
When nothing seems right
And I begin to lose sight
When I start to question
The black from the white
Like the root of a tree
Like the wind to my wing
Like a rock that shelters
Wild daisies in spring
When liquid snow flows
Along a brook gone dry
When a raindrop falls
And moistens the eye
You are there by my side
And yet not there…

A WINTER'S DAY

A winter's day:
Misty mornings
Clouded skies
Violet evenings
Silent nights;
Knitted feelings
Pine-tree logs
Fires roaring
Bulky gloves.

A winter's day:
A watery sun
And coffee cups
Currant buns
And roasted nuts;
Icy hands 'round
Steaming mugs
A frosty ground
And cheerful rugs.

A winter's day:
Feathery snowflakes
Buttery toasts
Languid lakes
Freezing toes;
Blue refrains
Knitted throws

Foggy panes
A frozen nose.

A winter's day:
Chrysanthemums
In cosy huts
And cardigans
All warm and snug;
Echoed sounds
Magnetic tugs
Homeward bound
And tender hugs.

It's a winter's day.

LOST AT SEA

Thoughts spill into words
Words drown out the pain,
My pen begins to falter
At sea and lost again.

Alone amidst a crowd
Mingled jumbled natter,
Lifeless conversations
Lost for words that matter.

Alone at the very top
Nobody shields awhile,
No one to say I care
No one to share a smile.

A life of paradoxes
Circuitous and oblique,
Stuck inside a maze
Lost again at sea.

WHERE IS LIFE TAKING ME

An enchanting time
In a charming place
A song in the air
Harmonious space
On top of a hill
The world below
The sky my pillow
The sun aglow
My soul a-tango
With radiant flowers
Silver oaks glow
Beneath the stars
A rainbow spans
Midsummer's June
My feet a-jingle
To a piper's tune.

Where is life taking me?

As time journeys on
I go where it goes
Along infinite roads
I go with the flow
Through highs of life
And through the lows
In pleasures and pain
And blooms and blows

Time races faster
My strides are slow
Innumerable lanes
And miles to go
I pause to marvel
As I rest a while
How far I've travelled
And the remnant miles.

So where is life taking me?

AS YOU WILL

You know I will
Do as you will
And your will will
Guide me through;

I know you will
Stay by my side
Wherever I am
Whatever I do;

Your gentle eyes
And sunny smile
Your tender touch
Like morning dew;

Your loving care
Flows in my veins
Fresh and fragrant
I smell like you;

Stay by my side
Don't go away
Give me a hand
As you always do;

Over hill and vale
Come walk with me
O Mother of mine
I'm a fragment of you.

COSMIC PRESENCE

Sometimes
When things go wrong
And dusk slips into night
The rain is incessant
No haven is in sight.

A lyric in the air
A warm gentle breeze
A tender cosmic touch
A rustle of the leaves.

Sometimes
I get a feeling
Although I'm on my own
You stand there beside me
I know I'm not alone.

IF ONLY...

If only
You and I
Could visit
Once again;
Moments
Lost in time
Of harmony
And of pain;

If only
We could hear
The resonant
Rich refrain;
It's faint with time
Yet audible
As the echo
Still remains.

If only
You and I
Just hear
Each other out;
The chasm
Between us
Deepens with
Every word we shout.

If only
Truth prevailed
And vanquished
Deception's clout;
Much water's flown
And changed us
From within and
From without.

If only
You and I
Patched up
Our differences;
Lived a life
Worth living
And rose
Above ourselves;

If only
We could grow
Beyond our
Cramped fences;
If remnant
Distant dreams
Glossed over
Stubborn stances.

If only...

LAZY SUNDAYS

A slow lazy Sunday
Languid and laid back
The dog has a swag
His tail a constant wag.

Slow placid moments
There's music in the air
Faint aroma of shampoo
And glossy damp hair.

Buttery steaming toasts
With crosswords and coffee
Flowers below my window
Among butterflies and bees.

Slow languorous mornings
The day just whizzes past
The sun is on a scamper
The clock runs rather fast.

Before I catch my breath
The day is almost done
The leisurely pace is over
And Sunday's on a run.

It's time to get all set
The lazy air to pack
Forget the sunny Sunday
The frantic haste is back.

SIBERIA

It's as cold as ice
My mind is numb—
My toes are frozen
Each nerve is strung;
Can't move, can't think
Can't hold a pen right—
Can't sit, can't stand
Too cold to write.

It's as cold as ice
The pathways freeze—
A piercing wind
On glacial leaves;
Icicle danglers
Adorn the trees—
Snow-white flakes
A numb blue breeze.

It's as cold as ice
North winds blow–
Ice cold words
On a page of snow;
Grey drab clouds
A fogged up window—
Iced Russian smiles
Of frozen indigo.

It's as cold as ice
The skies are grey—
The mist is dense
Can't see the way;
So far from home
So far away—
Fly frozen bird
Show me the way.

It's as cold as ice
Come let's fly—
Let's spread our wings
And soar up high;
The sun will glow
Our wings will dry—
We'll forget the cold
As we reach the sky.

It's as cold as ice
In the world below—
The sun on my face
In my heart and soul;
Over the mountain
Across a meadow—
We're homeward bound
Beyond the rainbow.

It's as cold as ice
My mind is numb—

My toes are frozen
Each nerve is strung;
Can't move, can't think
Can't hold a pen right—
Can't sit, can't stand
Too cold to write…

THE LAST VERSE

As the sky turns red
As the sun goes down
As the earth is drenched in rain;
As evening falls
As the day is done
It all comes back again.

It's all over now
Nothing left to say
And the last verse
Ebbs away…

As leaves turn brown
As the winter comes
As the trees turn bare and cold;
As the world stands still
As the years goes by
The untold sagas unfold

It's all over now
Nothing left to say
And the last verse
Ebbs away…